Ballads of the Alone

ALSO BY RUPERT M LOYDELL

POETRY
Leading Edge Control Technology
*Wildlife**
The Fantasy Kid
*Boombox**
Lost in the Slipstream
*An Experiment in Navigation**
Ex Catalogue
The Smallest Deaths
*A Conference of Voices**
Familiar Territory
The Museum of Light

INTERVIEWS
*Encouraging Signs**

COLLABORATIONS
On Revelation Drive [with Alan West]
A Music Box of Snakes [with Peter Gillies]
Serviceable Librettos for the Deaf [with Nathan Thompson]
Memos to Self [with Nathan Thompson]
Overgrown Umbrellas [with Peter Dent]
Risk Assessment [with Robert Sheppard]
Make Poetry History [with Luke Kennard]
Shaker Room [with Lee Harwood]
Snowshoes Across the Clouds [with Robert Garlitz]
Eight Excursions [with David Kennedy]
The Temperature of Recall [with Sheila E. Murphy]
A Hawk into Everywhere [with Roselle Angwin]

EDITOR
Smartarse
*From Hepworth's Garden Out**
Troubles Swapped for Something Fresh
Voices for Kosovo
My Kind Of Angel: i.m. William Burroughs

*published by Shearsman Books

Rupert M Loydell

Ballads of the Alone

Shearsman Books

First published in the United Kingdom in 2013 by
Shearsman Books
50 Westons Hill Drive
Emersons Green
BRISTOL
BS16 7DF

Shearsman Books Ltd Registered Office
30–31 St. James Place, Mangotsfield, Bristol BS16 9JB
(this address not for correspondence)

www.shearsman.com

ISBN 978-1-84861-310-2

Copyright © Rupert M Loydell, 2013.

The right of Rupert M Loydell to be identified as the author
of this work has been asserted by him in accordance with the
Copyrights, Designs and Patents Act of 1988.
All rights reserved.

Acknowledgements

Some of these poems have previously appeared in *A Conference of
Voices* (Shearsman Books), *The Eternal Anthology #3* (Raunchland),
Stride and *Poetry Salzburg Review*.

Ballads of the Alone and *Different Chemistry* were first published
as illustrated limited editions by Utopian Compensation. *Multiple
Exposure* was first published as an illustrated e-book online by
Shearsman. *Wallflower* was first published as an illustrated
pamphlet by Nightshift.

Thanks to Randolph Healey at Wild Honey, Larry Marshall at
Utopian Compensation, Tony Frazer at Shearsman, and to Harvey
Hix for his introduction. Also to Peter Dent, Mike Ferguson, Thomas
White and Clark Allison for correspondence about these poems, and
for unknowingly helping with the blurb.

Cover photo by the author.

Contents

Introduction by H.L. Hix	7
1. Ballads of the Alone	15
2. Multiple Exposure	29
3. Wallflower	43
4. Different Chemistry	57
5. A Product of Negotiation	71
Sources	86

Rupert Loydell's
Ballads of the Alone

Contemporary poetry is not alone—it has the good company of contemporary visual art, contemporary classical and jazz music, dance, nowadays even literary fiction—in being often ignored, dismissed, or shied away from on the grounds that it is 'difficult'. But that shying away indicates a misunderstanding at work: new poetry *is* often difficult, but not in the way 'difficult' is usually meant.

Something might be difficult in any of various ways: as chess is difficult (so nearly infinite in its complexity that it evades mastery), as climbing Mount Everest is difficult (physically demanding, dependent on extensive preparation and support), or as a calculus problem is difficult (susceptible to solution only by application of specialized knowledge and technique). Something might be difficult as playing the 'Moonlight Sonata' is difficult (contingent on talent honed by years of training and practice), as a spoiled child is difficult (demanding, belligerent, self-absorbed), or as a thoroughbred is difficult (high-strung, obstinate).

The contemporary poetry you hold in your hand, Rupert Loydell's *Ballads of the Alone*, is difficult, but not in any of those ways. A clue to what "difficult" means in application to Loydell's work comes from its etymology. The English word "difficult" originates in the Latin compound of the negative prefix *dis-* and the root *facilis* ("easy"). Simply following that root back into English signals the sense of "difficult" that best suits Loydell's work. It is *disfacilis*: i.e. it is *not facile*.

What is facile fulfils convention without resistance. Genre fiction (such as the mystery or romance novel) offers countless examples of the facile. If I read a mystery novel, I know before I buy the book exactly what to expect and when to expect it: a crime, probably a murder, will be committed early on, a detective will be called in to solve the crime, and so on. I even know when to expect the unexpected: I expect to be surprised by the revelation of the murderer's identity, when the detective reveals that, and how, the clues point to someone other than the person to whom I thought they pointed.

In contrast, what is *disfacilis*, difficult in the sense that *Ballads of the Alone* is difficult, may employ conventions but will also, even *in* its employment of them, resist them. One set of conventions especially prominent in relation to *Ballads of the Alone* is that of *ekphrasis*, the description or evocation in poetry of another work of art. Surely the best-known example of ekphrastic poetry in English, John Keats' 'Ode on a Grecian Urn', typifies the conventions of ekphrasis: description of the object in terms deferential enough to justify the attention paid it, leading up to an edifying synthesis, even a moral. Loydell draws on, or appeals to, ekphrastic conventions, but does so less to fulfil them than to challenge them.

The first element of Loydell's challenge to convention is his having chosen subjects and sources that themselves both employ and resist convention. Consider the photographers named as the subjects of Loydell's ekphrasis.

The first sequence here, 'Ballads of the Alone', is composed, Loydell notes, "after W. Eugene Smith," to whom writer and photo historian Geoff Dyer attributes a "dementia of seeing" (163). In Loydell's sequence, the dementia of seeing assumes various identities: a "carnival logic of urban dreams," "pictures in musical order" (as compared, for instance, to narrative order), "dislocations," "stolen and borrowed voices" gathered not into a choir over which the singular will of a conductor rules but into a party through which an overhearer may wander, tasting conversation after conversation. Dementia imposes a gap between memory and experience, signals a mind's withdrawal from correspondence into coherence.

The second sequence, 'Multiple Exposure', is "after Aaron Siskind". Peter Turner describes Aaron Siskind's work as "abandoned, mutilated leavings of man and nature, seen suspended in an inescapable dimension; forward movement blocked by surface, retreat into perspective no longer allowed" (n.p.). The "abandoned, mutilated leavings" in Loydell's poems indicate "a fascination with fragmentation" that "looks like it says something" even though "you never know just what it means". Loydell's repeated end line, "balance of time as well as form", resonates against the "no longer" in Turner's description of Siskind. Loydell's leavings, like Siskind's, draw us into "an older more essential world", densely inhabited but differently animated than our own, in which "there is only absence".

Loydell's third sequence, 'Wallflower', is "after Ralph Eugene Meatyard and Deborah Turbeville". Noting a contrast between the typical family photograph and the photographs of Meatyard, which depict family members wearing masks, Elizabeth Siegel says, "The family snapshot is always in 'directorial mode'—*hold still, say cheese, look over here*—to construct an ideal reality". But with a twist in Meatyard's photographs, Siegel notes, because "he controls the scene not to manufacture familial flawlessness, but to create mystery, trigger emotional associations, and encourage second looks" (128). Franca Sozzani says of Turbeville: "When Deborah takes pictures every single detail is perfect yet wrong at the same time. She doesn't look for perfection but for casual order—her order. Unconventional" (7). Loydell's unconventionality becomes a "soft focus view through broken glass", and his control of the scene creates "strangers from invented time". #12 of 'Wallflower' includes a description that a reader could take as referring to the speaker of the poem: "a man alone in a reinforced cage / collaging quotes and screams".

'Different Chemistry', Loydell's fourth sequence, is "after Joel-Peter Witkin", who Eugenia Parry describes as portraying "the human figure as a repository of abjection", a mode of portrayal that takes us to a "frontier" beyond our conventional self-understanding: "What is base and contemptible", she says, has in Witkin's work "the power to forge a frontier beyond the body; the abject shows us the borderline of our condition as living beings in order to provide the means by which we are able to lose ourselves, our 'I,' symbolically, as witnesses to the horror, and in the process, recreate and restore ourselves" (n.p.). The frontier beyond the body in Loydell becomes "a different kind of space" that is nevertheless, as the repeated last line of each poem in this sequence has it, "the condition of our lives". The abject becomes in Loydell "the dark poetry by which we live", poetry because it invites/incites recreation of ourselves, dark because it witnesses the horror, the loss of ourselves.

Finally, 'A Product of Negotiation', the concluding sequence, is "after Edgar Martins and Marco Breuer". Andrea Aversa says of Martins that "the flow of information usually deriving from a photo is replaced... by interpretations. Through his process of disrupting our expectations of the image, Martins challenges judgments that are based upon what is perceived as 'real' or 'fake'."

In Loydell, the disruption that undercuts the distinction between real and fake also sabotages any certainty: over and over in the repeated last line of each poem, I can only *think* I have arrived. "I think I have arrived" leaves more than one thing uncertain: the place, the arrival, the journey. Even I myself am made uncertain. Transformations become uncertain, and "it is not what it seems" becomes true of *any* "it".

What I am trying to suggest is that the choice of ekphrastic subject, once complemented by the reciprocity that in composing the poems Loydell establishes between the photographers' work and his own, establishes a dialogue that can be continued in reading the poems. He is not so much pointing out lessons his subjects teach us ("Beauty is truth…") as venturing in his chosen medium experiments analogous to experiments they ventured in theirs, and thus inviting *us* to recapitulate—and to stretch or contest—those experiments. In other words, the choice of convention-challenging subjects occasions further challenges to convention, in process of composition, in "form" and "content" of the poems themselves (as if those were separable), and in their 'personal' and "political" enactments as reading (as if *those* were separable). As a result, "the poem forces us to expand our boundaries of what we think of as meaningful" (Bruns, 27). *Ballads of the Alone* does not merely *collect* its fragments as (in Heraclitus' formulation) "a heap of random sweepings", but *arrays* them as a realization on the page of the "biological operation" in the brain that Barbara Maria Stafford claims is "akin to the rhetorical function of analogy" and is "responsible for the synaesthetic convergences of discrete information distributed all over the brain occurring when we think coherently" (212). Thinking coherently, in other words, may be more *distributed* than localized, more arrayed than sequenced, more shuffled than hierarchized, more combinatory than monumental.

To borrow the words of David Mutschlecner, Loydell's book is a "sapient / concatenation: / language braided with creation" (83). As words combined in relation to a linguistic grammar may result in discovery, so may fragments combined in relation to a "grammar of collage". *Ballads of the Alone* demonstrates that from attention to the made a moral or lesson (a *facile* and localized encapsulation of wisdom, a bromide) is not the only form of edification, nor beauty the only value, nor simplicity and transparency the only form of invitation. Loydell takes us in these poems "to see // reason at the point of exhaustion / fragmented and polarized". His is a difficult vision, not a facile one. *Ballads of the Alone* presents "a landscape of uncertainty", but reading it leads me to say what it says: "I think I have arrived".

H.L. Hix

H. L. Hix's most recent book is a "selected poems" entitled *First Fire, Then Birds: Obsessionals 1985-2010*, and his forthcoming poetry collection is *As Much As, If Not More Than*. His books of criticism and theory include *Lines of Inquiry, As Easy As Lying*, and *Spirits Hovering Over the Ashes: Legacies of Postmodern Theory*. He earned his Ph.D. in philosophy from the University of Texas at Austin, and currently teaches in the Philosophy Department at the University of Wyoming. His website is: www.hlhix.com.

Works Cited

Aversa, Andrea. 'Edgar Martins at Betty Cuningham.' *Art in America* 95:5 (May 2007): 198.
Bruns, Gerald L. *The Material of Poetry: Sketches for a Philosophical Poetics*. Athens, GA: Univ. of Georgia Press, 2005.
Dyer, Geoff. *The Ongoing Moment*. London: Vintage, 2007.
Mutschlecner, David. *Enigma and Light*. Ahsahta Press, 2012.
Parry, Eugenia. 'Convalescent… Incorruptible.' Introduction to *Joel-Peter Witkin*. London: Thames & Hudson, 2008.
Siegel, Elizabeth. 'The Universalizing Mask.' Afterword to *Ralph Eugene Meatyard: Dolls and Masks*. Radius Books, 2011.
Sozzani, Franca. 'Foreword.' *Deborah Turbeville: The Fashion Pictures*. London: Rizzoli, 2011.
Stafford, Barbara Maria. *Good Looking: Essays on the Virtue of Images*. Cambridge, MA: MIT Press, 1996.
Turner, Peter. 'Aaron Siskind. Photographer.' In *Aaron Siskind: Photographs 1932-1978*. Museum of Modern Art (Oxford) and A. Zwemmer Limited, 1979.

Ballads of the Alone

'A photograph is a secret about a secret, the more it tells you, the less you know.'
      —Diane Arbus

'I know how forgetting & photography make grief possible'
      —Joshua Marie Wilkinson

1. Ballads of the Alone

after W. Eugene Smith

'Is the man walking into the dark or the light?'

1

towers shift down to abstract image
flames and sparks engulf a man
umbrella vase web x-ray zebra
a fragile child held still and poised
your wife will get old but not mine

time-warped doubt coherently mapped
carnival logic of urban dreams
jelly king lion mouse necklace
reading deeply into the texts of others
there is no way to the surface

hope will be merely a straw man
exposure is just the starting point
elephant fish goat hedgehog
shrewd self-preservation (legend pales)
stark contrast between dark and light

2

hunt through deserted corridors
slammed glass doors always shatter
goluptious gondola goitre gone
frustrated circulation and movement
reverse the orientation of matter

instant packaged exhibitions
and immediate comprehension
gorgeous gorget goodness goon
each monument an encounter
one more useless scrap of metal

prepared to enter is no trap at all
forms of resistance can end
gonfalon gopher godetia gong
gallery wall and cool white fluorescence
stark contrast between dark and light

3

lampshade hanging from a wire
pictures in musical order
untitled interior installation
desperate utopian compensation
ex-wife's new home in the suburbs

the rhythms of the city change
change by being repeated
untitled untitled hot-roll steel
filamented lines and textures
arranged in a receding space

a drink and something to eat
a triangle between two roads
plywood untitled exterior
no mention of photography
stark contrast between dark and light

4

long moments of sheer beauty
no chance of us returning
gas stations   funeral parlours   motels
a misguided group of electrons
criss-crossing both sidewalk and street

pools of light and streams of silk
almost medical intimacies
shoulders   buttocks   arms   scuffed elbows
huge scale, glossy close-ups
accompanied by extended captions

the toolshed of childhood
secrets kept as long as could be
friendship   madness   passion   death
stolen and borrowed voices
stark contrast between dark and light

5

past the gift shop and reception
ready to abandon time
casual silence   early nights
thinking about warm water
breathing into airless lungs

ripping up carpets and settling in
a series of private meetings
marriages   friends   past lovers   children
the world out back transfigured
no less than a second honeymoon

hand clamped over mouth
memory frosting over
glacier   rockfall   frozen sea
white noise of repression
stark contrast between dark and light

6

radio stations as instruments
how we eat our young
telephone   scissors   perimeter fence
find me some new sounds
re-shape, re-order everything

simmering becomes boiling
from gas to solid to liquid
correction   collapse   reversal
we all rolled down our windows
as the past rode up to talk

the king of the island
became what had been dream
ladder   ocean   orchard
the man who brings assertion
stark contrast between dark and light

7

god of the wind and rain
whirling rush of spinning earth
damask   morocco   sandgrain   plain
floods scooping hollows in the rock
distant ridges still on fire

sharp-eyed curiosity
journeying across the map
ridged   ripple   stipple   cord
contemplate lost specimens
despair lined up along the road

only imagine what will follow
self-cancelling perception
brocade   coltskin   linen   lined
strategies restoring power
stark contrast between dark and light

8

dislocations such as this
explain intricacies of belief
bokhara   vermillion   forest   birch
memories of familiar objects
dust spinning out behind

intimacy and confused love
I tend to go a little misty
emerald   medina   tabriz   tan
no respect for nothing
all our lives are now in doubt

premonitions of disaster
travelling high vibrating lines
pristine   oatmeal   vellum   mist
tiny flowers and fragile timbers
stark contrast between dark and light

9

a breeding-place of wind and drift
difficulty turned into song
kestrel fulmar sparrow dove
all the foghorns in the world
kilowatt hour by kilowatt hour

weaving through the debris
history apparently consumed
skylark tern flamingo thrush
high winds and pressure drop
dwellings on a hillside

I stand in need of explanation
images taken for granted
bullfinch plover lapwing kite
a passionate exercise in faith
stark contrast between dark and light

10

swept along by wind and tide
welcome guests to the evening
smoke scarlet kraft pearl
no time at the end of the world
how did you track me down?

a crowd of about two hundred
complained in thunderous voice
pink damascus citrine stone
a series of stylized tableau
the glove signifies the hand

contradict the new disorder
tortured and distorted flesh
sapphire violet maize fern
I am taking apart the genius machine
stark contrast between dark and light

11

walking upright from the forest
corridors between makeshift rooms
trout sturgeon cisco pike
portraits stare down from the walls
threatened with extinction

park the car off the public highway
is this the way to paradise park?
squawfish pupfish minnow chub
moving along the invisible road
not with prayers but slogans

dramatic close-ups and bleaching techniques
interference between stations
darter gambusia wetjaw toad
scratching and digging for a living
stark contrast between dark and light

12

proverbial swing of the pendulum
flashbulbs popping in the night
waffle   warble   wanton   ward
a man without hands pounding glass
fed up with lying in state

back to the moment of explosion
we need no explanation
whether   weather   weasel   warm
opposition seems to be shifting
the phone lines always adrift

negotiations breaking down
extolling the virtues of war
warrior   warrant   wheedle   weep
diagonal movement out of the frame
stark contrast between dark and light

2. Multiple Exposure

after Aaron Siskind

'It has to do basically with bringing order into our life.'

1

asphalt sparkles with energy
on the shoulder of the highway
insipid plankton thermal hoof
inner tensions transform the image
swing and tilt between two planes

a fascination with fragmentation
language and lettering on city walls
trumpet weasel electric poise
it looks like it says something
you never know just what it means

pleasures and terrors of levitation
opposing forces held
lark denial vital sources
we can only see the shadows
balance of time as well as form

2

the exhilaration of uncertainty
slow shutter speeds achieving blur
turret   nostril   gugtupper   wilt
a reflection of basic duality
only implied by surface

delicately repeating shadows
falling across an unlocked door
buzzer   velvet   diffident   swoosh
all my possessions in a suitcase
stone doorstep become a home

reality seen as dappled abstraction
wounds and healing, experience, age
pilchard   goldsmith   billabong   beak
vital symbols of life and change
balance of time as well as form

3

memory's continuous imagination
more than ever I feel alone
definition plummet grimace cleave
things we try to forget are there
laid out cold on the front lawn

a certain corner of the dancefloor
the missing centre of the sign
ovary frankness forensic drift
how does it feel to hit the wall?
the rest of the body is worn away

last drops squeezed from a dirty rag
betrayal of the people
ostrich acquaintance coracle launch
doors and windows flung wide open
balance of time as well as form

4

private feeling or actual happening
welcoming batch of diverse events
serenity fissure percussion wrap
impossible questions well worth asking
the hobgoblin of little minds

find the asylum before it shuts
our factories are closing down
incidence binomial puncture twist
there was all the time in the world
past is now a lump in the throat

we all crave the caress of the voice
desire approval of the ear
waterfall slipper wheelbarrow tryst
somewhere else just out of sight
balance of time as well as form

5

I could show you my passport
how to get to there from here
tangent   router   herring   slump
the idea of a map or songline
truth in circumference and in form

criss-cross and open-endedness
nothing left for us to find
ubiquitous   mallard   vibration   spoon
cutting back and weeding out
we are forever walking

man made a journey to the stars
I have not gone so far
admittance   walnut   muck   deceit
mysteries, dreams and superstition
balance of time as well as form

6

industry working around the clock
how drab and sham it gets
luminous urge adhesion chord
history is fascinating in itself
explained past provokes our doubt

sound quality of imagination
posthumous blueprint for applause
nutrition banter fillet tern
distant view of zinc-grey waves
a window into another time

I am complicit in betrayal
dazzled by acts of being kind
wingtip incursion hypnosis proof
assert the value of the present
balance of time as well as form

7

being inspired turning a corner
whatever suits expressive needs
snorkel   tunic   social   pike
muffled in our waterproofs
our fires have been extinguished

incidental friends and furniture
the slow advance of science
cordial   extremity   sealant   clip
community of enlightenment
cosmic tunes and heavy tax

an older more essential world
threshold of heaven reached
intransigent   basic   contortion   melt
ceaseless dance of ambiguity
balance of time as well as form

8

cooking breakfast over a fire
further from home than you
helical   compassion   disqualified   hound
suburb to the vanishing point
transient images of our town

here there is no sodium haze
the evening sky glows green
invisible   marmoset   daffodil   proof
part of a large invisible system
devils with snakes for hair

the aeroplane falls slowly
through a tangle of briars
cerebral   trouser   palladium   milk
sudden shimmer of light and leaves
balance of time as well as form

9

another set of ruined buildings
ghosts of structures such as these
inculpate   query   sausage   tilt
bridges, girders, lines and chains
a peculiar perspective

light brown coat in case of rain
a favourite of my father's
cornflake   wrestler   resurgence   monk
drifting fog among dripping pines
living worlds of mutual trust

a sort of shrinking into life
phantom pains within my chest
volcanic   upright   belligerent   jump
sheets of paper blackened with print
balance of time as well as form

10

hundreds of forgotten pictures
sometimes layered deep
exclamation   register   irrigate   chime
overheard rooms empty of noise
transparent moments such as these

love shows itself minute by minute
in ways that are easy to doubt
inverse   armature   liquorice   cheese
alcohol has dulled its progress
formation dancing in the tide

the midday sun is strengthening
gravity become too much
cucumber   traffic   fearless   grill
there is only absence in the world
balance of time as well as form

11

a long night of unsettled weather
gulls above rise high and scream
spider illusion crocodile scar
lighter patch on hill's steep slope
clouds ahead of a silent storm

stood there in a kind of trance
minimal movement and pressure
sidegarnet filcher horology graft
stumbling over secret words
remembering my real name

the backs of terraced houses
girls dancing in the street
persecute porcupine salient cheek
prettily built and fully glazed
balance of time as well as form

12

places we'll never visit again
a small trapdoor in the floor
miltweeker prophecy indulgence clamp
echoes cancel each other out
water gone quiet in pools

inside talking about money
outside shouting at snow
navigate backbill repertoire lurch
elevator doors beginning to close
chance ringing of church bells

he takes that rucksack everywhere
presses the shutter release
morphism physics nylon savant
learn to love light as well as dark
balance of time as well as form

3. Wallflower

*after Ralph Eugene Meatyard
and Deborah Turbeville*

'my pictures walk a tightrope'

1

painting declared to be dead
subject almost accidental
eggplant consumption almanac duke
found to be alive again
deserving of attention

sidelong or lazy glances
acts of understatement
charlie samba intestine towel
red fingernails grown too long
eroticize the landscape

visible elements of time
geometric stylization
platinum furbish suntan yowl
all the people have now gone
memory of something seen

2

I don't have a camera
I want to make a film
talisman   agate   waddle   cope
in the greenhouse frizz and perm
peeling paint and ancient stone

crumpled fabric on the floor
suggests a woman's height
anglican   distillate   cranberry   snick
absurd game of hide-and-seek
a kind of invitation

images you want to keep
vapourized by sunlight
airline   reversion   enzyme   blurt
pack up and get out of here
memory of something seen

3

blue light   snow light   twins and trees
recurrent syncopations
rectory   sickroom   sideband   talk
blaze of bracken   pleats and tucks
autumnal oatmeal clothing

scratchy prints and greasy lens
drapes on someone's sofa
whitlock   darkle   mustang   crop
black kohl eyes and hennaed hair
cardboard boxes tied with string

velvet dresses dragged through dirt
mannequins and models
winter   keyhole   downgrade   prim
soft focus view through broken glass
memory of something seen

4

striking features   drafty halls
beauty in new clothing
avalanche   resin   cubbyhole   boot
excuse me I don't want to dance
desire half understood

bodies in the freezer
held in contorted poses
magpie   supine   baseline   wheel
conspiracy may be afoot
amnesia and neuroses

a kind of moody restlessness
more fiction than fact
buried   rowboat   buckhorn   mate
absence to be grateful for
memory of something seen

5

chew your fingers   suck your hair
pose against the wall
elaborate giddy denizen stale
frozen space   erotica
stay hidden in your room

muted understatement
no image of herself
gangster bonnet schoolgirl roof
shattered mirrors   silver shards
reflections of contempt

beautiful puppet features
needing a name or place
paperweight invite contaminate book
strangers from invented time
memory of something seen

6

jump-rope songs and bawdy rhymes
strange machines and flying saucers
feather continuum decorate swing
a magic circle drawn in ink
hush of a dark window

people sent around the world
their own fantastic spaces
spatterdock token mahogany jibe
emerging into light too harsh
clutching the past about them

distant music   ringing bells
a little out of tune
mandrake arcade forestry din
soundtrack of angelic song
memory of something seen

7

monuments and steel towers
strange idea of a city
deadlock participant contingent swarm
traffic patterns   eyes and ears
impromptu dance and theatre

apologetic prayer flags
hung on flimsy sticks
utopian addict breastplate rune
tomorrow is a one-way trip
the past another day

dark stripes   tyre tracks in the snow
curved steps in hard-edged shadow
candlelight vandal melamine state
making it up as you go along
memory of something seen

8

isolated mausoleum
rent always months behind
comeback   tussle   playmate   breeze
look at the corpse in the cold
and wonder where you've been

repetition and repeat
life's low grade mechanics
floodlight   turtle   dreamboat   wave
half-hearted prayer   posture of grace
belief's elastic creed

hollow-eyed skull in the cupboard
a template for death when it comes
cockroach   proscenium   confiscate   brawl
the life you save may be your own
memory of something seen

9

fantasy is self-comfort
waiting outside the door
vector departure masquerade fugue
one old hand gripping another
love no longer our home

this is no amusement park
just the same old skin
signpost homeland ambassador squint
over the island into the river
assassination team

out of my mind on photography
not knowing what to do
bakelite tattoo carrion wave
the creative action of decay
memory of something seen

10

remember the stranger I never met
his mock-confessional tone
fibrosis pigeon undulate clone
walking the streets for no good reason
day unfolding like a dream

flirting with likeable images
only one passion back then
waxwork mouthful headland page
the camera a way to hold conversation
breath and wind the very same thing

further along the spiritual path
speaking only in your own words
toothpaste beachcomb embellishment tang
choose one direction or another
memory of something seen

11

squinting at the morning sun
everything in flames
soprano bypass petroleum realm
phone numbers safe in my pocket
light floods along the hall

shooting at others to stay alive
always on the wrong side
paradigm centaur lumbar gloat
every day the fat guard speaks
I forget I am never alone

the emotional release of mourning
the power to make death go away
curlicue shoofly cholera drop
a chance to tell a great story
memory of something seen

12

magical textures of light engross
firefly showers sparkle and gleam
tilt   procession   acetate   spade
I am practising improvisation
breaking all my own rules

the voiceless with drum and banners
lies and slogans on tv
conserve   confessor   padlock   lathe
a man alone in a reinforced cage
collaging quotes and screams

dying here would not be useful
you're too good-looking for that
firepower   azimuth   hypocrite   fact
the pain of trying to retrieve the past
memory of something seen

4. Different Chemistry

after Joel-Peter Witkin

'I'm alive and I'm in need'

1

still lifes   still deaths   living corpses
grotesque wounds & sepia stumps
try again   trying not to
too much talk makes me nervous
short cuts through both truth & dream

missing limbs & phantom phallus
masks & cloaks for costume balls
too many words   too overpowering
freakshow   circus   party
we might as well address it now

semen   spittle   broken head
meat & gristle   dimestore mask
transfixed   traumatic   transformation
explores a different kind of space
the condition of our lives

2

there are no stars   there is no sky
everyone is scarred
luminous   made my morning
cold luxurious finished print
no evidence of life

we should all live naked
characters in an unmade play
too dark   too right   too serious
comic-book gothic backdrop
morbid dirge-rock bands

moral codex in our hearts
an unsure kind of faith
nonsense nostalgia numinous
I can't make judgements clearly
the condition of our lives

3

doomed to making photographs
allowing their own resonance
morbid   miserable   meaningful
received request again this time
ignoring the above

excellent condition
limbless man tied to a bed
reality   relax   remind
blindstamped title   no colophon
give comfort to the dead

intellectual camouflage
transparent head of fire
banal beating   atmospheres
marks & shapes   foreground & space
the condition of our lives

4

fruit around a baby's corpse
disguising things that hurt
excellent excellent extra
fearless image-maker
never drops the mask

blurry timeless image
scratched tissue paper fuzz
endless enticing everyone
silence does the talking here
another kind of work

being disciplined she burnt it
starts the whole process again
expansive eye candy explode
accepting the unquestionable
the condition of our lives

5

yes to everything possible
no to the diseased past
I laughed   I left   I love you
cut with surgical precision
there's no proof after that

going to cross the horizon
manipulate the past
I swear   I stare   I question
silent & not moving
objects held and thrown

rays of light a saving grace
caged in basement pain
I'm sure   I'm there   I'm sorry
between depravity & the divine
the condition of our lives

6

words taken out of context
the content of the work
gooseflesh garbage genuine
the list is getting longer
stories about glass

a short cut to the image
scab memory of a cut
horrible horrible honesty
flesh & fluid landscape
beyond all cold debate

a metaphor for everything
the oldest person left
complex constant contradict
stop scowling at the audience
the condition of our lives

7

sleeping spirits from the past
mannequins & deformed dwarfs
inane inept indecision
victim of a drowning
accidental birth

breathing spells & memories
dreamt I saw your face
slightly sometimes previous
fearful deviant hellishness
severed at the knee

stilted exchanges overheard
conversations in the dark
listen listen liked them
slumped amid abundance
the condition of our lives

8

dead eyes staring upwards
beaten silvertone
you can't   you don't   you shouldn't
dysfunctional & wretched
images as prayers

transfiguration on the table
non-omniscient gaze
you did   you will   you mustn't
a sideshow for the curious
collapsed by closing time

being there without going
these visual lies are true
you see   you've seen   you realise
reaching for eternity
the condition of our lives

9

the list is getting longer
language of the dumb
lifelike   limit   lithesome
these are rocks from childhood
this my state of mind

excess engenders repulsion
decay reveals the past
meticulous   morbid   marvellous
the sacred love of mother & child
the beauty of serpentine

blink & you'll miss the sun in your eyes
stand outside & scream
drama   dramatic   devalued
rise above this world of pain
the condition of our lives

10

interlude   no one home
pale skinny corpses
decorative   doubt   desirable
I might not be paying attention
enigma wears thin in time

razor blades   pins & needles
relics of unknown saints
intricate   intimate   insane
this is the result of war
the confusion of the now

photographs of mirrors
drawings of the self
sympathy   stamina   stigmata
begin by going back again
the condition of our lives

11

a short cut to the image
the peace I'm trying to find
stranger suicide subordinate
animals & their redeemer
a dance of solitude

dissected face veiled in lace
charged power relationship
who says why bother will you
polished blood & rusting steel
green cloth in grey slipcase

the things we might remember
outside photographic time
fiction fraught made final
no proof at all that I did that
the condition of our lives

12

the spiritual centre of secular life
sometimes there's a doubt
wonder   wishful   wisdom
I want your flesh gone blue & grey
to set up home with me again

wanderers in the desert
body parts in blocked-up drains
wouldn't   would have   wouldn't
difference & tolerance
two jailbirds crushing stone

these bodies are just thrown away
brains sometimes put back in
wacko   weirdo   worst in show
the dark poetry by which we live
the condition of our lives

5. A Product of Negotiation

after Edgar Martins and Marco Breuer

'How do I know what I know
until I see what I see?'

1

Edgar, your work baffles me
imperfect circles of light
slice   abrasion   colour shift
each box houses its own surprise
continues to record

pan & tilt the present tense
all emotion now excised
wind turbine   pylon   watermill
jagged pixilations
how image makes itself

sound baffles on a highway
no post-production work
radio mast   aerial
a terse passage of dialogue
I think I have arrived

2

darkness croak & slither
impressions of various times
moon-addled   canny   circumspect
thick fog in empty studio
hidden inner spark

bluer skies & crisper light
vegetative greens
low level entry   boarding ramp
evocation of the sublime
against a scrim of smoke

transformed from a field of scars
into radiant terrain
urban   suburban   periphery
chilled with tragic presence
I think I have arrived

3

the running blur of a movie
the lesson incomplete
astute   mischievous   blasé
fleeting shadow on a wall
an instruction of signs

hidden layers of blindness
radiating from a void
temperature   pressure   wind speed
near white-out combinations
ice floes that levitate

image becomes meditation
tied to people, place & things
airport   corridor   underpass
all about temporal experience
I think I have arrived

4

emptied out approximations
tricks of scale which confuse
hand-drawn circles   grace & poise
results rather than process
beautiful useless things

fingered, creased & smudged
mishandled & abused
glasspaper   file   sandblast
sensitive to emulsions
the quality of glass

tonal & textual comparisons
the runway & the sea
relentless flight   obsession
technical transformation of sound
I think I have arrived

5

moves toward decomposition
evaporation of a dream
metaphor   movement   moment
opportunity slighted
illusion remains all

installations in darkened rooms
landscapes that survive
departure   destination
interstitial spaces & voids
capturing what is gone

these two lines would double again
strange attractors look so strange
passport   passage   pathway
new ways of making pictures
I think I have arrived

6

poking around secondhand stores
for jettisoned intimacies
namesake   distance   memory
trying to overcome it
no theatre there at all

I work with long exposures
not the obvious kind
radius   centre   ring road
downright anachronistic
the way we deal in lies

rehearsal & performance
well-placed wrong ideas
concept   balance   story
always something going on
I think I have arrived

7

complex tools for understanding
recording passages of time
gesture   pinprick   self-contained
a steady stream of water
between the tap & sink

fluorescent signs & markings
memories that bridge the void
utopia   rigour   nuance
rehearsing one's own exclusion
achieving the sepia tone

a landscape of uncertainty
a fleeting & powerful somewhere
mapping   memory   monsoon
one can be grabbed without knowing
I think I have arrived

8

extended moments of action
free of mirrors & surprise
interest   intrusion   ideal
special access self-service
no clear beginning or end

pitted, scratched & pockmarked
punctured, smoked & singed
strategy   strangers   stormclouds
looking up a blackened valley
forgotten peace & quiet

further detail comes into view
joints & hinges move
technique   tension   tactile
a fixed & constant condition
I think I have arrived

9

I'm tempted to be interested
not allowed to make a noise
autism   asbo   audit
the concept needs rethinking
muttering broke out in the hall

pay attention to the silence
channel thoughts & ideas
business   buskers   boom & bust
uncertain transformations
it is not what it seems

it's not easy to make a photograph
not easy to break your fall
benefit   branding   bottom line
the burden of representation
I think I have arrived

10

passages quoted from a notebook
renegotiated terms
contract   confuse   no comment
speedy access to information
a world of flux & flow

I know about godlike responses
unbelievably cute first words
daddy   mummy   eggbox
each & every construction
polymorphic & multiform

optical memory elements
history is being made
traverse   reverse   mirror
the doppelganger is introduced
I think I have arrived

11

sorry-owled & frivolous
half-baked & broken-limbed
surveillance   shelter   shortage
blown-fused critical comments
debate is taking place

primed with a sense of purpose
a photography of ideas
surveillance   shopping   strip mall
minute tonal differences
difficult to decode

a primitive kind of theory
suspended disbelief
surveillance   probation   problem
the unwanted sound of everything
I think I have arrived

12

new ways of urban planning
the complex taken to extreme
welfare whitewash wipeout
abnormal periodic order
there's nothing wrong with you

give form to invisible process
this is the way it's done
power performance pedagogue
incomplete science & skewed presentation
we had the misfortune to see

reason at the point of exhaustion
fragmented & polarized
chaos catalyst chasm
the future will never happen
I think I have arrived

Sources

BALLADS OF THE ALONE: *Bookforum*, Fall 2001; *A Friend of the Earth*, T.C. Boyle; *Performance Art*, RoseLee Goldberg; 'Through the Crash Barrier', L.J. Hurst; *Minimalism*, ed. James Meyer; *Beyond the Frozen Sea*, Edwin Mickleburgh; *Another Roadside Attraction*, Tom Robbins; *W Eugene Smith* [Phaidon 55 monograph]; *Joel-Peter Witkin* [Phaidon 55 monograph]; *Arcana*, ed. John Zorn.

MULTIPLE EXPOSURE: letter from Clark Allison; *Ars-Interpres* #1; *Don't Ask Me What I Mean*, eds. Clare Brown and Don Paterson; *The Cryptographer*, Tobias Hill; *Sea Room*, Adam Nicolson; *Austerlitz*, W.G. Sebald; *Aaron Siskind* [Phaidon 55 monograph]; *Heaven*, Peter Stanford; *Ocean of Sound*, David Toop; music lists by wetbicycleclappersoup.

WALLFLOWER: *Fools Rush In*, Bill Carter; *JG Ballard*, Michael Delville; 'Where have all the people gone?', Michael Glover, *The Independent* 9 January 2004; *Motherless Brooklyn*, Jonathan Lethem; *The Second Coming*, Antony Lopez; *Ralph Eugene Meatyard* [Phaidon 55 monograph]; *Ezra Pound. The Pisan Cantos*, ed. Richard Sieburth; *Think of the Self Speaking. Harry Smith—Selected Interviews*; *Wallflower*, Deborah Turbeville.

DIFFERENT CHEMISTRY: *Witkin*, Germano Celant; 'Joel-Peter Witkin, "Harms Way... lust & madness, murder & mayhem"', derkeiler.com; *Peregrination: Conversations with Contemporary Artists*, Robert Engright; *Hamish Fulton* [catalogue]; *Red Shift*, Alan Garner; *David Hiscock* [catalogue]; 'Death grins on Joel-Peter Witkin, "patron saint of the weird"', Amie Johnson; *Worth the Trip*, Low Profile; *A Fine Anger*, Neil Phillips; 'Joel-Peter Witkin', Michael Sand; 'Joel-Peter Witkin', Cintra Wilson; 'Joel Peter Witkin—the New Pope of Photography', Cindy Marler; *The Bone House*, Joel-Peter Witkin; *Joel-Peter Witkin* [Phaidon 55 monograph]; *Joel-Peter Witkin* [Thames & Hudson Photofile]; 'Masters of Fine Art Photography: Joel-Peter Witkin'.

A PRODUCT OF NEGOTIATION: *Early Recordings*, Marco Breuer; *Eleven Times James Brooks*, James Brooks; 'Old Boy', Jenny Diski, *LRB* 19 Aug 2010; *Italian Hours*, Henry James; *Topologies*, Edgar Martins; *when light casts no shadow*, Edgar Martins; 'How can I see what I see, until I know what I know?', Edgar Martins [www.edgarmartins.com]; *Ground Control*, Anna Minton; 'Rain, Blow, Rustle', Nick Richardson, *LRB* 19 Aug 2010; *Chaos for Beginners*, Ziauddin Sardar & Iwona Abrams; *Sinister Resonance*, David Toop.

Biogaphical Notes

RUPERT LOYDELL is Senior Lecturer in English with Creative Writing at Falmouth University, and is a poet, painter, editor and publisher. His books include the Shearsman titles *Wildlife* and *Encouraging Signs*, a collection of interviews, conversations and essays, as well as many collaborative texts, and *The Tower of Babel*, an artist's book-in-a-box. He currently lives in a small creekside village in Cornwall with his family, records and books.

H. L. HIX's most recent book is a "selected poems" entitled *First Fire, Then Birds: Obsessionals 1985-2010*, and his forthcoming poetry collection is *As Much As, If Not More Than*. His books of criticism and theory include *Lines of Inquiry, As Easy As Lying*, and *Spirits Hovering Over the Ashes: Legacies of Postmodern Theory*. He earned his Ph.D. in philosophy from the University of Texas at Austin, and currently teaches in the Philosophy Department at the University of Wyoming. His website is: www.hlhix.com.